I0502651

THE GUIDE TO GETTING STARTED

"any deal, any size, any location"

Nathan Tabor

Copyright © 2018

All rights reserved. No part(s) of this book/guide may be reproduced, stored in a retrieval system, or transmitted in any form or by any means, electronic, mechanical, photocopying, recording, scanning, or otherwise without the prior written permission of the publisher.

Table of Contents

Define Your Niche

Imagine walking into an ice cream shop and saying, "I would like some ice cream." What is the FIRST thing the person behind the counter is going to say? Simple. "What flavor?"

Telling others you are a "real estate investor" has the same effect. It doesn't define you or what you do. It actually creates more questions in a person's mind.

When describing your niche, you must be specific like this: "Nathan Tabor is a real estate investor who focuses on Class C apartment complexes with major deferred maintenance and occupancy issues." That is MY niche.

Accurately defining your niche is critical. If you simply tell someone you want to purchase real estate, they aren't going to buy in to your plan. In their mind, they are probably thinking this person has no real concept of what they want to do.

4 Steps to Defining Your Niche

I found my niche. And you can find yours too! My niche is class C apartment complexes with serious, deferred maintenance issues and extremely low occupancy. Truth be told, if you don't find your niche in life, you won't be content and satisfied. Likewise, if you don't find your niche in real estate, you will waste a lot of time and energy.

Step One:

The biggest factor in finding your niche is determining how much money you have for a down payment. Banks currently require an average of 10-20% down.

So, ask yourself these questions: How much money do you have or how much money can you raise from investors? For example, if you can have or can raise $20,000 and the bank requires 20% down then you can do a $100,000 deal. If you have $100,000 then you can do a $500,000 deal and if you have $200,000 then you can do a $1,000,000 deal. This is a crude, but realistic example.

Step Two:

Establish what you want to achieve and define your goals out in writing.

Are you trying to complete one project per year while keeping your current job? Or is your intent to strike out on a full-time venture?

This is extremely important because the world of real estate is vast with so many different options, you can spend all your time chasing deals but never acquiring or finishing one.

I have one "friend" who started flipping at the same time I did. As of January 2017, he still hasn't flipped a deal but is still trying. One month he is working on a $50,000 deal, and the next time I hear from him, he is working on a $20 million-dollar deal.

When you don't have a clear objective you normally don't get much done.

Step Three:

Determine the ideal location of your investment(s).

Should you invest close to home or invest in another market? If your plan is to be involved in all aspects of the project, you'll want to live closer to the property. If your plan is to buy in another market, make sure you have the infrastructure to handle what's needed on a day-to-day basis.

Step Four:

Determine which class of real estate you will pursue. Are you looking for a lower, but safe return? Then property that is considered "Class A" is your market. A "Class A" piece of real estate will give you the most security, but it also gives you the lowest return.

Whereas, a "Class C or D" property will give you a greater chance at profit but comes with a higher risk. My greatest successes occurred when taking D+/C- deals and bringing them up to C/C+ properties.

Create Your Business Plan

Being Focused Is Critical

Growing up in Northern Alabama was an incredible experience for me. The community was poor, but nobody knew it because everyone had what they needed—and everyone in the community helped each other.

As a child, I didn't spend much time inside. We lived outside almost year-round. From riding horses to playing hide-and-seek to painstakingly digging holes in the middle of an abandoned field, we were always outside.

The activity and the outdoors kept us in good shape. And at the same time, being outside from sunup to sundown served as a method to stimulate our creative juices.

I'll never forget the time the "one-eyed god" became an issue. My brothers and I caught the television bug and started sitting around watching TV more than spending time outside. We had even started to neglect helping our mother around the house, which made her none too pleased.

Distractions can happen in our lives from time to time. We know very well that we should be doing other things, but some other will takes over. Why? The new activity could be less stressful, it could be more fun, or we could simply be procrastinating. The reason doesn't really matter, however. What matters is recognizing the idleness, standing up, and snapping out of it.

Eventually we told our mother we would do just that. And we did… for a short time. Then we went back to our old ways of watching TV. This cycle of activity and inactivity went on for several months until my mother had finally had enough. She walked into the den, unplugged the TV, and proceeded to cut the cord in half with a pair of scissors! He announced that if we couldn't get done what needed to be done on our own, she would leave us no alternative.

So, the moral of this story is that if you have something in your life that is holding you back from achieving what you need to achieve, then it's time to cut the cord! And when the time is right, you can come back to the activity and enjoy. Truth be told, it was four years until our mother allowed us to watch TV again. And you know what? We didn't miss it one bit!

The Importance of a Business Plan

Not having a business plan is like taking a family vacation without making any plans. If you show up to the airport on the day you want to travel, you may or may not get a flight. If you do, it could cost you more than you planned. You might have to wait several hours to board an available flight. Or maybe you could miss the flight by thirty minutes because you didn't get there on time.

If you do get on a flight then, where are you going to stay once you arrive at your destination? And if you leave your wallet and driver's license behind, what will you do then?

So, you don't just wake up on a Monday morning, jump in your car, and start driving to a destination. If you do, others will think you have NO common sense. NO purpose. NO vision. NO organization.

This is what an investor or bank thinks when you don't have a detailed, specific business plan. The business plan is your official roadmap, and it has all the necessary details of how you are going to fund and operate your business.

Your detailed business plan establishes your niche. This single document is your greatest asset in securing an investor or bank financing. You need to spend a great amount of time, thought, and research while writing your business plan. Then you'll need to work hard to refine it… and then refine it again. The result should be that anyone should be able to read your business plan in about 10 minutes and know exactly what you want to accomplish and how you plan to get there.

The number one benefit of having a business plan is to create a roadmap or step-by-step plan for yourself. Your business plan forces you to focus on and develop your primary message and identify your specific niche. The sooner you can clarify your message and niche, the sooner your business will take off.

CRITICAL TIP:

I highly encourage you to consult a business professional or mentor in helping to write your business plan. There are hundreds of ways to write a business plan, so, the following information should server as a good starting point.

The number one rule when writing a business plan is NOT to make it a fluff piece. Make it realistic and honest. After all, if you fudge the details on the report, you're only lying to yourself. And accurate roadmap to success will get you there a lot faster than one filled with falsehoods and half-truths. For example, if you state that you want to start flipping real estate and plan to have a $20 million portfolio within two year, that isn't realistic. Could it happen? Sure! Anything can happen. Is it the norm? Absolutely not. Let's look at the necessary elements of a business plan.

Executive Summary

The Executive Summary is the most critical and important part of your business plan. It is the hook that will keep someone — a banker, an investor, a business partner — reading. Your Executive Summary serves as an overall summary of who you are and what you want to do. It is a 10,000- to 30,000-foot look at the path ahead.

The subsequent parts of your business plan allow you to expand on your executive summary. I find it prudent to leave the executive summary for last because it's hard to summarize the topics you have yet to cover. Once you gather and report all the information below, you can simply take the highlights of each section and combine them to build your Executive Summary.

Some sections can be paragraphs or even pages long, but it's ok if some of these sections contain only one or two sentences. Include details, but don't be boring. After all, you are telling a story, and you want it to be a compelling story. Do NOT chase rabbits! Meaning, focus on what your goals are and the help you need to accomplish your goals.

Company Description

Describe your company's legal structure, mission statement, vision, goals, and target market.

Market Analysis

There will always be properties to buy, renovate, flip or keep. The true issue will be finding the deals that fit your business model. Research the market; pull comps (comparables) by working with a local real estate broker or using a website like loopnet or zillow.

Organization & Management

Do you have other parties involved in your business? If so, this is where you list their name(s), title(s), responsibilities, and prior experience.

This is also where you discuss the management of your company. Who's going to manage renovations? Who's going to manage rentals? Who's going to list the properties? You can address items like working with licensed contractors or performing the work yourself. The more detail the better.

Positioning/Niche

Define out exactly what you want to do, where you want to do it, how you are going to do it. If you want to focus on duplexes, then describe how it will be accomplished. If you want to purchase strip malls or single family or purchase raw land this is where you do it.

Funding Request

Now it's time for the big ask. You'll need to detail how much money you are requesting and exactly how you plan to use it.

What terms you are offering? If you're certain about what you can offer, then go ahead and include that in your funding request. However, I would suggest omitting this information so you can negotiate the terms as you go.

CRITICAL TIP:

Acquiring an investor is 10 times easier if you have real property to show them. It is easier to say I need $20,000 to purchase, renovate, and flip the property located at 123 South Main Street than it is to get funding for the next deal you might find.

It is also hard to find a property if you don't know if you can find an investor. If you are in this situation, then I recommend taking the following actions:

- Pull comps on 3-5 flips in the area.
- Build out an investment packet based on these numbers.

Once you have your investment packet prepared, and then start seeking investors. Show them the packet. Then ask them if you can find these types of deals, how much would they invest? Once you have solid commitments from investors, and then go find the property. Finding the right property WILL take a lot of hard work and diligence no matter how you put your plan together.

Immediate Steps to Take

Develop your plan. Be honest with yourself. Where are you now? Where do you want to be? What are you willing to sacrifice to get there? Once you have this written, convert it into a plan of action.

Be diligent with your plan. Review your plan often. Discuss it with others. Research the best ways to reach your goals. Ask questions. Turn over every stone. Stay on top of your plan and when a problem arises address it immediately.

Deliver your plan. Confidence and passion are important in reaching your goals. Be ready to share your vision with others. Remember, only YOU can achieve your goals! (But you might need the help of others along the way.)

Don't fear failure. Fear being in the exact same place next year as you are today! - unknown

How to Create an Investor Packet

In my opinion, it is better to NOT have an investor packet than to have a horrible one or one that is has missing information. An investor packet that is properly constructed will help you with your bank and investors.

Here are a few tips to keep in mind when creating your investor packet:

- The potential of the deal is the most important element.

- The design of the packet needs to be professional.

- Make it easy to read and follow.

- Create a hook. Why this deal is too good to pass up?

- Share the backstory of the property. Provide details about how it got to this condition.

Elements of an Investor Packet

Cover Page

Provide all relevant information on the cover page. It is basically the index page of a book. Items to include on the cover page:

- Property photo

- Property name and address

- Property asking price

- Property cap rate or comparable value

- Your name and contact info

This page highlights the deal and isn't for promoting your business.

Property Highlights

Bullet point the benefits of the deal:

- Purchase price

- Renovation costs (if needed)

- Completed value after stabilization

or

- Amount of Net Rent

Tell your potential investor why this is such a good deal. There is a value-add play, it has good schools, in a good neighborhood or whatever you think is important.

Property Photos

You can take the photos yourself or get them from the listing broker. You can also typically find images through an internet search or from the tax card.

Just remember two things:

- The better the photos, the better the packet.
- All photos should be realistic in case your investor visits the property.

Have you ever looked at a property online and it looked amazing until you drove by the property? There is a HUGE powerline system right beside the property or a junk yard. Game over.

Location

List the property address here again and take a screenshot of a Google map. It is important to describe the area and any possible amenities: proximity to dining, entertainment, parks, venues, etc. For example, there is a grocery store 0.7 miles from the property. If the investor is on the fence with the deal, the location may either help or hurt.

Also detail the property's proximity to local roadways, intersections, businesses, and any other relevant information.

Financials

The type of property will determine what you put in here. Cash flow is going to apply to commercial and multifamily. Comparables will apply to single family.

Current Cash Flow Analysis

Provide documentation that supports what the property is currently collecting (Rent Roll) as well as the current expenses. To determine the property value, see the Cap Rate section in Chapter 12.

Projected Cash Flow Analysis

How long will it take to stabilize the property? What will the property collect once it is stabilized? What are the projected expenses? Plan to build out this section and thoroughly explain your numbers.

Think you can raise rents each month? Explain why. For example, the current rent is $100 under market rate. There are five complexes within a two-mile radius that rent for $600 a month and the current rent for your property is only $500 per month.

Comparables

Research the market; pull comps (comparables) by working with a local real estate broker or using a website like loopnet or zillow. If you do the research by yourself, you might have to pay to have an account.

Renovations Needed

Detail how much money will be invested in renovations, what renovations will occur, and how long it will take to complete the renovations.

Area Description and Market Data

This section becomes more relevant as the dollar amount of the project grows. Here are some questions you'll need to answer in this section:

- Where area of town is the real estate located?

- What are the financial demographics?

- Is the crime in the area going up or down?

- What are the employment trends in the area?

- Are businesses creating new jobs or losing jobs?

- Who are the major employers in the area?

- What are the population growth trends?

- What are the area vacancy rates?

Most of this information can only be found by paying for a service or working with a real estate broker.

This structure is the primary foundation for your investor packet. However, as you work with different investors on a deal, you may find that you need to add or delete other elements.

This section is not needed but the more information you include the more comfortable an investor will be with the deal.

Disclaimer Notice

You need to add a disclaimer notice on your investor packet. You always need to add a disclaimer to anything you do. If you don't know if something is legal, then contact an attorney for confirmation. Many investors have found themselves tied up in legal issues, so be sure that you're doing everything by the book before you get started.

Bonus: Getting Started Without Money

What can you do if you don't have money or can't raise money? There is still HOPE!

Get Creative!

The bottom line is that if you are determined to be a real estate investor then go ahead and do it! It may be what you think you want now. And it might not be the path you want in the end. Or success and money might not come as fast as you want. But as with anything else in life worth achieving, obtaining your dream most likely isn't going to be easy and it will take a lot of sweat equity, hard work, and determination on your part.

So, if you don't have money to start your project and you can't find an owner to provide owner financing or give you an option to buy, there is still another idea: become an expert!

Become a property manager. Learn the business of marketing, leasing, collecting rent, filing evictions, turning units and writing plans. This experience will give you a working knowledge of the ins and outs of managing and maintaining real estate.

Become a handyman or contractor. From how to purchase materials, how to hire contractors and how to do the work yourself. Learn the ropes, learn how to save money, learn how to make yourself invaluable to the process.

Become an apprentice. Find a management company, contractor or investor who needs a right-hand person. Learn their trade. Listen to how they conduct business. Surround yourself with people who are smarter than you. Then listen to their experiences, take their advice, and follow through.

Just know upfront that you aren't going to be handed your dream on a silver platter. But know that if you want it, you can make it happen!

CRITICAL TIP:

Be careful! If you take over management, maintenance or rehabilitation of a property and give the owner your personal guarantee, you can be liable if you default. These steps should be taken after you have done your due diligence.

About Nathan Tabor

Nathan Tabor has built a life helping others and improving lives. Throughout his own life and experiences, Nathan has acquired an incredible ability to solve problems, develop game plans, and create real and lasting results in both his personal and professional life.

He has successfully founded and operated more than two dozen businesses since 1999, grossing over $150 million in sales. His experience spans the areas of commercial real estate acquisition and redevelopment, automobile sales, direct product sales, web-based marketing, and strategic partnership facilitation.

Real Estate Experience

- 26 Properties Flipped in 9 years

- Grossed over $52 million in sales

- Raised over $1 million from investors

- Consulted on deals worth over $200 million

- Author, The Guide to Due Diligence

- Author, The Guide to Defining Your Niche

- Author, How to Find, Finance, Fix & Flip Apartments

- Author, Achieving Balance

He's had amazing successes and epic failures, and learned more from his failures than his successes. After years of struggling to keep all of the balls in the air, he learned that there are laws and processes that, when implemented, will deliver the desired results.

Over the years, his companies have been honored with many awards and rankings. In 2012, 2013 and 2104 his parent company was ranked by Inc. magazine's Inc. 5000 as one of the fastest growing small businesses in the United States. In 2014, 2015, and 2016, his real estate management company was listed as one of the largest in the Piedmont Triad.

Nathan earned his Bachelor's degree in Psychology from St. Andrew's Presbyterian College and his Master's degree in Public Policy from Regent University. He has been married to Jordan since December 2003 and their daughter Abigail was born in January 2005.

Services Offered

No matter your real estate goals — buying, selling, renovating, securing funds or flipping — as an experienced and knowledgeable consultant, I will help bring opportunities into focus and develop a plan of action. You'll gain the experience, know-how, and strategic planning to help you avoid the many pitfalls of the real estate business. And you'll take away actionable items that you can implement in your business today!

Services offered:

✓ Brainstorming session: This is a one-hour session with Nathan designed to answer and/or discuss any topics. Ranging from where you should start or how to deal with a specific issue.

✓ Coaching: Nathan will walk you through a series of exercises from setting your goals, developing your business plan to expanding your business.

✓ Consulting: From finding a deal, engaging a real estate broker, structuring a deal, approaching an investor, submitting a loan request to any part of a real estate deal Nathan can assist you.

✓ Work-Life Balance Program: As you know, it's critical for people to have a healthy work-life balance. That means managing your professional life alongside your personal life in a healthy way. Why? Because stress and anxiety affect a person's ability to function at their best.

✓ Analyzing Deals: This involves all aspects of the deal ranging from reviewing the purchase contract, rent rolls, comps, expenses and leases to analyzing the P&L's, comps and cap rate. Nathan will then provide you with a report identifying any areas of concern. Finding an error or correcting an error can swing your deal by tens of thousands if not hundreds of thousands of dollars.

✓ Flipping Deals: Nathan will help you package your deal to take to market. First impressions matter the most. The strength of your packet sets the tone for negotiating the sale.

✓ Finance/Refinance: There are numerous options available: Construction Loans, Acquisition Loans, Cash

Out Refinance, Renovation Loans and many other options.

✓ Due Diligence: Don't have the time to walk every unit or worried you might miss something? Nathan can help you will a particular part of due diligence or he can do all of the due diligence for you.

Interested in working with Nathan? Send an email to Nathan@NathanTabor.com

Disclaimer

All material contained in this book is provided for educational and informational purposes only. No responsibility can be taken for any results or outcomes resulting from the use of this material. While every attempt has been made to provide information that is both accurate and effective, the author and publisher do not assume any responsibility for the accuracy or use and/or misuse of the information herein. The author and publisher do not guarantee that anyone following these techniques, suggestions, tips, ideas, or strategies will become successful. The author and publisher shall have neither liability nor responsibility to anyone with respect to any loss or damage caused or alleged to be caused directly or indirectly by the information contained in this book.

www.ingramcontent.com/pod-product-compliance
Lightning Source LLC
Chambersburg PA
CBHW030740180526
45157CB00008BA/3255